GW00319368

The NO MEAT Cookbook

Meat-free meals are a growing trend. Most households sit down several times a week to a meal minus meat, and whether the motivation is healthy eating, budget beating or a commitment to a vegetarian diet, it makes sense to have a repertoire of recipes which are based upon pasta, pulses, dairy products and vegetables.

This is not primarily a vegetarian cookbook, although vegetarians will find many delicious dishes within its pages. It includes several stunning recipes for fish and seafood. Fish is a valuable source of protein and vitamins A and D; white fish has a low fat content and even oily fish like mackerel is low in saturated fat.

The aim has been to provide a wide range of recipes for every occasion, from dips and nibbles to serve with drinks, to casseroles and hearty bakes for all the family.

Pulses such as dried beans, peas and lentils are good, inexpensive sources of protein, and, as such, belong in every pantry.

The variety and versatility of pasta makes it the perfect basis for a no-meat meal, whether as part of a simple stir-fry or layered with vegetables in a tasty lasagne. Rice also appears in many different guises, including risottos and pilafs. There are also a selection of recipes utilizing less familiar grains like couscous and barley.

CONTENTS

SOUPS FOR ALL OCCASIONS	2
TASTY SNACKS AND STARTERS	10
FABULOUS FISH AND SEAFOOD	18
NOURISHING RICE, PULSES AND GRAINS	22
PLENTIFUL PASTA	42
INDEX	48

SOUPS FOR ALL OCCASIONS

Served with warm crusty bread, soup makes a wholesome meal whatever the weather. On the following pages you will find a host of delicious ideas suitable for winter or summer, with recipes ranging from traditional favourites such as French Onion Soup or Asparagus Soup, to more unusual combinations such as Courgette Soup with Curry Puffs or Fresh Pea Soup with Radishes.

Pimiento and Tomato Soup

2 tspn olive oil

1 onion, finely chopped

500g (1lb) canned pimientos, drained and chopped

500ml (16fl oz) vegetable stock

2 tblspn tomato purée

2 tspn caster sugar

1/2 tspn grated nutmeg

30g (1oz) low fat cream cheese

1 tblspn arrowroot mixed with 2 tblspn water

1 tblspn chopped fresh dill for garnish

1 Heat the oil in a medium frying pan, add the onion and pimientos, and cook for 5 minutes.

2 Add the stock, tomato purée, sugar and nutmeg, cook for a further 5 minutes. Purée the pimiento mixture and cream cheese in a blender or food processor for 3 minutes, then rub mixture through a sieve into a large saucepan.

3 Add dissolved arrowroot to pan and cook mixture over moderate heat, stirring constantly until slightly thickened. Serve hot, garnished with dill.

Serves 3-4

Lentil Soup

280g (9oz) dried lentils

1 onion, finely chopped

3 sticks celery, finely chopped

2 cloves garlic, bruised

2 bay leaves

2 litres (3½pt) water

60ml (2fl oz) dry sherry

salt

freshly ground black pepper

1 Soak the lentils in water for at least 6 hours. Drain. Place in large saucepan with onion, celery, garlic cloves, bay leaves and water. Bring to the boil, then simmer for 1 hour.

2 Remove garlic cloves and bay leaves from pan, then add sherry, and season with salt and pepper. If soup is too thick add some water and heat through before serving.

Serves 4

Jerusalem Artichoke Soup

500g (1lb) Jerusalem artichokes

30g (1oz) butter

500ml (16fl oz) milk

1 onion, sliced

1 clove garlic, crushed

1 tblspn flour

1 litre (1¾pt) water

60ml (2fl oz) double cream

1 tblspn chopped fresh parsley

1 tblspn snipped fresh chives

1 Peel and slice artichokes. Melt butter in a large saucepan, add artichokes and cook over gentle heat for 5 minutes.

2 Combine milk with onion and garlic in small saucepan, bring to the boil.

3 Add flour to artichokes, stir well, then gradually add the water. Bring to the boil, reduce heat then stir in milk, onion and garlic mixture. Simmer, covered, for 1 hour. Stir in the cream, parsley and chives, and serve.

Serves 4

Winter Soup

185g (6oz) butterbeans or cannellini beans

250g (8oz) leeks, sliced

45g (1½oz) butter

3 swedes, cut into 1cm (½in) cubes

1 small turnip, cut into 1cm (½in) cubes

3 tblspn flour

1.5 litres (2½pt) vegetable stock

3 tblspn chopped fresh dill

salt

freshly ground black pepper

2 potatoes, peeled and cut into 1cm (½in) cubes

155ml (5fl oz) soured cream

dill sprigs for garnish

1 Soak, then cook butterbeans or cannellini beans according to instructions on page 25. Drain.

2 In large saucepan sauté leeks in butter until soft, about 4 minutes. Add swedes and turnip, stirring in well. Reduce heat. Add flour, mix in well.

3 Add vegetable stock gradually, stirring constantly, then add dill, salt and pepper to taste. Bring to the boil, reduce heat, cover, simmer for 15 minutes.

4 Add potatoes and butterbeans or cannellini beans. Cover and simmer until all vegetables are tender, about 15 minutes.

5 Strain 250ml (8fl oz) of the hot soup into small bowl, combine with soured cream, purée until smooth. Gradually pour this purée back into soup, stirring constantly. Heat through, but do not boil again. Serve garnished with dill sprigs.

Serves 6

Parsnip and Coriander Soup

45g (1¹/₂oz) butter
1 onion, finely sliced
1 bunch fresh coriander
2 pears, peeled and chopped
2 medium potatoes, peeled and chopped
1kg (2lb) parsnips, cut into 2cm (³/₄in) slices
1.5 litres (2¹/₂pt) vegetable stock
salt
freshly ground black pepper
250ml (8fl oz) double cream

1 Melt butter in a heavy-based saucepan. Add onion, sauté until softened but not browned. Set aside 6 sprigs of coriander for garnish. Strip leaves from remaining coriander stalks. Add stalks to pan with pears, potatoes and parsnips. Cover and cook over gentle heat for 6-10 minutes.

Pimiento and Tomato Soup

2 Add vegetable stock and coriander leaves to vegetables, bring to the boil, then simmer for 20 minutes or until vegetables are tender.

3 Allow soup to cool a little. Purée in a blender or food processor until smooth. Season with salt and pepper. Serve in individual bowls, and garnish with a large spoonful of cream and a coriander sprig.

Serves 6

Kitchen Tip
Many of the soups in this section are puréed in a blender or food processor. Alternatively you can purée the soup by pressing it through a sieve with a wooden spoon. For a coarser texture, break up the vegetables with a potato masher.

Above: Adzuki Bean and Pasta Soup   Opposite: French Onion Soup

French Onion Soup

60g (2oz) butter

4 onions, finely sliced

2 tspn flour

1 litre (1³/₄pt) vegetable stock

125ml (4fl oz) white wine

8-12 slices French bread, toasted

60g (2oz) Cheddar cheese, grated

1 Melt butter in a large saucepan over gentle heat. Add onions and cook very slowly for 15 minutes until golden brown. Add flour and cook for a further 5 minutes, stirring constantly.

2 Increase heat to moderate, add stock and wine and bring to the boil, reduce heat and simmer for 10 minutes.

3 Sprinkle one of toast side with cheese and grill until cheese has melted. Place cheese toasts in a soup terrine, pour soup over and serve.

Serves 4-6

Fresh Pea Soup with Radishes

1 litre (1³/₄pt) vegetable stock

1kg (2lb) shelled peas

8 fresh mint sprigs

125ml (4fl oz) double cream

125g (4oz) radishes, very thinly sliced

1 Place stock, peas and 500ml (16fl oz) water in a saucepan. Season, bring to the boil, then simmer, covered, for 7 minutes.

2 Add 2 mint sprigs, simmer, covered, for a further 5 minutes, or until peas are very tender. Discard mint.

3 Purée peas and liquid in a blender or food processor until smooth. Sieve into a bowl. Allow to cool. Add cream, cover, refrigerate for at least 4 hours or overnight.

4 Serve soup garnished with radish slices and remaining mint sprigs.

Serves 6

Adzuki Bean and Pasta Soup

1 tblspn olive oil

2 onions, chopped

2 cloves garlic, crushed

2 pimientos, roughly chopped

125g (4oz) dried adzuki beans, soaked overnight and drained

1.2 litres (2pt) vegetable stock

90g (3oz) dried small pasta shells

125ml (4fl oz) red wine

¹/₄ tspn freshly ground black pepper

1 x 220g (7oz) can chopped tomatoes

2 tblspn tomato purée

1 Heat the oil in a medium frying pan over moderate heat. Add the onions, garlic and pimientos and cook for 3 minutes, set aside.

2 Place beans in a saucepan, cover with water and bring to the boil, simmer for 30 minutes, drain.

3 Place beans and stock to a large saucepan, and bring to the boil. and boil for 10 minutes.

4 Add the pasta, red wine, black pepper, tomatoes, tomato purée and onion mixture. Reduce heat and simmer for 15 minutes or until beans are tender and pasta is *al dente*.

Serves 4-6

Pumpkin Soup

Sweet Potato Vichyssoise

1kg (2lb) sweet potatoes

2 large leeks, sliced

15g (¹/₂oz) butter

1.5 litres (2¹/₂pt) vegetable stock

salt

freshly ground black pepper

125ml (4fl oz) double cream

1 bunch watercress, finely chopped

1 Preheat oven to 200°C (400°F, Gas 6). Bake sweet potatoes in their skins in the oven for 1 hour, or until tender.

2 Cook leeks in butter in a covered heavy-based saucepan for 5-6 minutes. Add half the stock and simmer until leeks are tender.

3 Cut sweet potatoes in half, scoop out flesh and place in a food processor or blender. Add leeks and stock to blender or food processor, purée until smooth. Return purée to pan. Stir in remaining stock, season with salt and pepper. Simmer for a further 5 minutes. Allow to cool, chill in refrigerator.

4 Serve chilled with a swirl of cream and a handful of chopped watercress in each bowl.

Serves 6

Kitchen Tip

Despite the name, sweet potatoes are not members of the potato family, although they may be used in a similar way. Usually elongated in shape with a yellow or pink-brown skin and yellow or orange flesh, they are widely available.

Pumpkin Soup

30g (1oz) butter

1 large onion, chopped

2 tspn ground coriander

1 large potato, peeled and chopped

500g (1lb) pumpkin, peeled and chopped

750ml (1¼pt) vegetable stock

¼ tspn grated nutmeg

125ml (4fl oz) double cream

chilli powder and snipped fresh chives for garnish

1 Melt butter in a large saucepan over moderate heat. Add onion, stir in coriander, cook for 3 minutes.

2 Add potato, pumpkin, vegetable stock and nutmeg and cook until potato and pumpkin are tender.

3 Transfer the vegetables and 375ml (12fl oz) of the stock to a blender or food processor and purée until smooth.

4 Add cream and blend for a further 30 seconds. Stir purée into remaining stock in pan. Reheat soup and garnish with ground chilli and chopped chives.

Serves 4

Courgette Soup with Curry Puffs

30g (1oz) butter

2 medium onions, chopped

6 medium courgettes, sliced

750ml (1¼pts) vegetable stock

250ml (8fl oz) milk

125ml (4fl oz) single cream

¼ tspn grated nutmeg

Curry Puffs

¼ tspn salt

½ tspn medium curry powder

45g (1½oz) butter

45g (1½oz) flour

1 egg, plus 1 egg yolk

1 Melt butter in large saucepan, add onions and courgettes, cook over moderate heat for 10 minutes. Add stock, bring to the boil, reduce heat and simmer until vegetables are tender.

2 Purée onions and courgettes with 250ml (8fl oz) of the stock in a blender or food processor until smooth. Add 125ml (4fl oz) milk, the cream and nutmeg, purée for 30 seconds. Stir purée into stock.

3 To make curry puffs: Combine remaining milk, salt, curry powder and butter in a small saucepan over low heat. Stir mixture until it boils, remove from heat and stir in the flour. Return to a low heat and beat constantly with a wooden spoon for 30 seconds. Remove from heat, cool for 5 minutes. Beat egg and egg yolk together with a fork and slowly add to curry mixture, stirring until smooth.

4 Bring a large saucepan of salted water to the boil, reduce heat to a simmer and cook teaspoons of curry mixture in the simmering water for 5-7 minutes or until puffs float to the top.

5 Serve soup topped with 3 or 4 curry puffs.

Serves 4

Courgette Soup with Curry Puffs

Cold Cucumber Soup

30g (1oz) unsalted butter

500g (1lb) potatoes, peeled and cubed

4 large cucumbers, peeled, seeded and diced

2 onions, chopped

1.5 litres (2½pt) vegetable stock

salt

freshly ground black pepper

300ml (10fl oz) natural low fat yogurt

1 bunch fresh chives, snipped, for garnish

1 Heat butter in a heavy-based saucepan. Add potatoes, cucumbers and onions, cover and cook over a low heat for 6-8 minutes.

2 Add stock and season with salt and pepper. Bring to the boil, then simmer for 15-20 minutes, or until vegetables are soft.

3 Set aside to cool a little. Purée in a blender or food processor. Refrigerate until chilled, stir in yogurt. Serve chilled, topped with chives.

Serves 8

Beetroot Soup

30g (1oz) butter

1 clove garlic, chopped

1 onion, chopped

500g (1lb) beetroot, peeled and chopped

3 carrots, chopped

1 small parsnip, sliced

3 potatoes, peeled and chopped

1.5 litres (2½pt) vegetable stock

salt

freshly ground black pepper

lemon juice

300ml (10fl oz) soured cream

1 Melt butter in a heavy-based saucepan, add garlic and remaining vegetables and cook for 10 minutes. Add vegetable stock, bring to the boil, cover and simmer until vegetables are tender. Add salt and pepper to taste, and a squeeze of lemon juice.

2 Purée in a blender or food processor. Serve hot or cold with a large spoonful of soured cream.

Serves 6

Gazpacho

4 tomatoes, peeled, seeded and chopped

1 onion, chopped

2 cloves garlic, crushed

1 small green pepper, chopped

1 small cucumber, chopped

500ml (16fl oz) tomato juice

1 Purée half the tomatoes with the onion and garlic in a food processor or blender until smooth.

2 Stir in green pepper, cucumber, tomato juice and remaining chopped tomato. Serve chilled.

Serves 4

Avocado Soup

2 ripe avocados, halved, stoned and peeled

155ml (5fl oz) natural low fat yogurt

1 tblspn lemon juice

185ml (6fl oz) vegetable stock

60ml (4 tblspn) single cream

Tabasco sauce

salt

freshly ground black pepper

1 tblspn chopped coriander

1 Place avocado, yogurt, lemon juice and vegetable stock in blender or food processor. Blend until smooth, pour into a bowl.

2 Stir in cream and Tabasco sauce, season with salt and pepper. Cover and chill for 2 hours. Just before serving, stir in coriander.

Serves 4

Kitchen Tip
The lemon juice in this soup will help to prevent the avocado from discolouring. Another way of stopping avocado from turning brown is to leave the stone in the purée, removing it just before serving.

Asparagus Soup

500g (1lb) asparagus

1.5 litres (2¹/₂pt) vegetable stock

pinch of sugar

15g (¹/₂oz) butter

1 tblspn flour

salt

freshly ground black pepper

grated nutmeg

strips of orange rind for garnish

1 Trim asparagus, peel if necessary, cut into 2.5cm (1in) pieces. Reserve tips.

2 Bring stock to the boil in a large saucepan, add asparagus, excluding tips, add pinch of sugar, cook until tender. Purée asparagus and stock in a blender or food processor until smooth.

3 Cook asparagus tips in a saucepan of lightly salted boiling water until just tender. Drain.

4 In a large saucepan melt butter, add flour, season lightly with salt, pepper and nutmeg and stir over a gentle heat for 1 minute. Gradually add puréed soup to pan, stirring constantly. Bring to the boil, reduce heat, simmer for 10 minutes, until soup has thickened.

5 Add asparagus tips, check seasoning and heat through. Serve garnished with strips of orange rind.

Serves 6

Kitchen Tip

It is not necessary to use the best quality asparagus spears for this recipe. Instead, look out for the thinner spears or sprue. This soup provides a good way of using a glut of the vegetable, and can be frozen for up to 3 months.

Gazpacho

TASTY SNACKS & STARTERS

Whether you want a sophisticated starter or a quick midweek snack, you will enjoy recipes such as Tomato and Basil Sorbet, Prawn Mousse, or Cauliflower Pizza.

Golden Fried Mozzarella

250g (8oz) mozzarella cheese

30g (1oz) flour

salt

freshly ground black pepper

2 large eggs

185g (6oz) dried breadcrumbs

375ml (12fl oz) groundnut or vegetable oil

1 Cut mozzarella into 1cm (1/2in) slices, then into 1cm (1/2in) strips.

2 Sift flour with salt and pepper into a deep plate. Beat eggs in another deep plate, spread out breadcrumbs in a third deep plate.

3 Dip mozzarella strips into flour first, then in beaten eggs, and finally in breadcrumbs, making sure strips are covered in crumbs completely.

4 Line a large baking sheet with nonstick paper. Arrange strips in one layer and refrigerate for 1 hour.

5 Heat oil in a frying pan, cook mozzarella strips in batches until golden on both sides, turning once. Drain on paper towels. Serve hot.

Serves 6

Spinach and Feta Filo Logs

125g (4oz) butter

1 onion, chopped

12 spinach leaves, chopped

2 eggs, lightly beaten

125g (4oz) feta cheese, crumbled

30g (1oz) grated Parmesan cheese

3 tblspn chopped fresh parsley

12 sheets filo pastry

1 Preheat oven to 180°C (350°F, Gas 4). Melt 30g (1oz) of the butter in a frying pan, add onion, stir over a gentle heat until tender, then remove onion. Add spinach to butter remaining in pan, cover, cook until softened. Drain spinach and squeeze out excess liquid. Combine onion, spinach, eggs, feta, Parmesan and parsley in a bowl.

2 Melt remaining 90g (3oz) of butter. Brush a sheet of filo pastry with a little of the melted butter, top with another sheet of pastry, brush with butter; continue until you have 4 sheets of pastry. Using a pair of scissors, cut into 4 rectangles. Place a heaped tablespoon of spinach mixture along the long side of one rectangle. Roll up, tucking in edges as you roll. Repeat with remaining pastry, butter and spinach mixture to make 12 rolls.

3 Place rolls onto greased baking sheets, brush with butter and bake in oven for 20 minutes or until golden brown.

Makes 12

Spinach and Feta Filo Logs

Onion Soufflé

30g (1oz) dried breadcrumbs

60g (2oz) butter

625g (1¼lb) onions, thinly sliced

1 tblspn snipped fresh chives

salt

freshly ground black pepper

2 tblspn flour

185ml (6fl oz) milk

4 eggs, separated, plus 1 egg white, at room temperature

1 Preheat oven to 200°C (400°F, Gas 6). Oil the inside of a 1.2 litre (2pt) soufflé dish. Add breadcrumbs and coat the inside of the dish evenly. Set dish aside.

2 Melt half the butter in a medium heavy-based frying pan over a gentle heat. Add onions and chives, season with salt and pepper. Cover and cook for 50 minutes until onions are very soft, stirring occasionally.

3 Melt remaining butter in a heavy-based saucepan over gentle heat, add flour and cook for 2 minutes, stirring constantly. Remove pan from heat, whisk in milk, return to moderate heat, whisk until boiling. Season with salt and pepper, reduce heat and cook, stirring frequently, for 5 minutes. Stir in onions.

4 Off heat, whisk in egg yolks one by one. Return pan to gentle heat and cook mixture gently, whisking constantly, until thickened.

5 Beat egg whites with a pinch of salt until stiff. Stir 2 tablespoons of the whites into the onion mixture, then fold in the remaining egg whites.

6 Spoon into the prepared dish, run your thumb along the top inside edge; this will enable the soufflé to rise more evenly. Bake for 20 minutes, or until well risen and lightly browned on top. Serve immediately.

Serves 4

Guacamole

2 ripe avocados

2 spring onions, chopped

1 ripe tomato, peeled, seeded and chopped

2 tspn chopped fresh coriander

2 tspn lemon juice

1/2 tspn chilli sauce

coriander sprig for garnish

1 x 200g (6¹/₂oz) packet corn chips to serve

1 Cut avocados in half, remove stones and scoop out flesh into bowl. Mash flesh with fork, then stir in spring onions, tomato, coriander, lemon juice and chilli sauce.

2 Spoon guacamole into a serving bowl, garnish with coriander and serve with corn chips.

Serves 4-6

Smoked Salmon Pâté

125g (4oz) smoked salmon

125g (4oz) cottage cheese

250g (8oz) butter

1 tblspn dry sherry

1 tblspn mayonnaise

1 tblspn lemon juice

freshly ground black pepper

Tabasco sauce

1 Blend salmon and cottage cheese in a blender or food processor until smooth. Melt butter over gentle heat, then add to salmon mixture and blend thoroughly again.

2 Add sherry, mayonnaise and lemon juice, blend for 30 seconds. Season to taste with pepper and Tabasco sauce.

3 Serve at room temperature with toast or crackers.

Serves 4

Guacamole

Tomato Sorbet

Dill Dip

1 tspn Dijon mustard
1 tspn white wine vinegar
2 tblspn olive oil
155ml (5fl oz) soured cream
2 tblspn finely chopped fresh dill
1 tblspn finely chopped fresh parsley
2 cloves garlic, crushed

1 Combine mustard and vinegar, then slowly add olive oil until mixture is well combined.

2 Add soured cream, dill, parsley and garlic and season to taste. Mix well and serve cold accompanied with florets or sticks of raw fresh vegetables like cauliflower, courgettes, carrot and fennel.

Serves 4

Tomato Sorbet

375ml (12fl oz) tomato juice
2 tblspn tomato purée
3 tblspn chopped fresh basil
2 tspn freshly squeezed lime juice
1 tspn Worcestershire sauce
1/4 tspn freshly ground black pepper
basil sprigs for garnish

1 Combine the tomato juice, purée, basil, lime juice, Worcestershire sauce and pepper; mix well. Freeze mixture in 2 ice-cube trays until solid.

2 Remove sorbet from freezer 5 minutes before serving. Serve garnished with basil sprigs.

Serves 2

Beetroot Timbales with Mustard Dill Sauce

1 x 454g (14¹/2oz) jar baby beetroot, drained and chopped

300ml (10fl oz) double cream

4 eggs, lightly beaten

lemon slices and beansprouts for garnish

Dill Sauce

60ml (2fl oz) soured cream

1 tspn mild mustard

2 tspn chopped fresh dill

1 Preheat oven to 180°C (350°F, Gas 4). Purée beetroot. Pour 250ml (8fl oz) of the purée into a medium saucepan. Reserve remaining purée for another use.

2 Stir 125ml (4fl oz) of cream into purée, stir over a high heat until mixture boils. Reduce heat, simmer for 5 minutes; cool for 15 minutes.

3 Whisk beaten eggs into beetroot mixture and pour mixture into 4 greased, 125ml (4fl oz) timbale tins. Cover with foil and stand in a roasting tin. Pour in boiling water to a depth of 2cm (³/4in). Bake timbales for 45 minutes.

4 To make sauce, bring remaining cream and soured cream to the boil in a pan, cook until mixture is reduced by a third. Stir in mustard and dill and serve with the timbales.

Serves 4

Crunchy Chickpeas

375g (12oz) cooked chickpeas (see page 25)

60g (2oz) butter, melted

1 Preheat oven to 200°C (400°F, Gas 6). Combine cooked chickpeas in baking dish with melted butter. Shake dish so all the chickpeas are well coated.

2 Bake 1 hour or until chickpeas are crisp and golden. Cool, season with salt to taste.

Serves 6

Beetroot Timbales with Mustard Dill Sauce

Prawn Mousse

375g (12oz) cooked, peeled prawns cut into 1cm (¹/2in) pieces

¹/4 small cucumber, cut into small cubes

4 tblspn lemon juice

3 tblspn white wine vinegar

1 tspn horseradish sauce

salt

freshly ground black pepper

4 tspn powdered gelatine

60ml (2fl oz) water

125ml (4fl oz) double cream, whipped

185ml (6fl oz) mayonnaise

1 Combine prawns, cucumber, lemon juice, vinegar and horseradish sauce in a bowl, season to taste with salt and pepper, leave to marinate for 30 minutes.

2 Sprinkle gelatine on to cold water. When spongy, melt over hot water, cool slightly. Stir gelatine, cream and mayonnaise into prawn mixture; taste for seasoning.

3 Rinse 4 small moulds in cold water. Pour in mixture, chill for 4 hours or overnight until set. To unmould, briefly dip moulds in hot water and turn out onto serving plates. Serve with dry biscuits.

Serves 4

Hummus

750g (1¹/2lb) cooked chickpeas (see page 25)

3 cloves garlic

5 tblspn tahini (sesame seed paste)

6 tblspn lemon juice

salt

freshly ground black pepper

olive oil

3 tblspn chopped fresh parsley

1 Combine chickpeas, garlic, tahini, lemon juice and salt and pepper in a blender or food processor, blend until smooth and thick.

2 Pour into serving bowl, drizzle some olive oil over the top and garnish with chopped parsley. Serve with pitta bread triangles.

Serves 6

Kitchen Tip
It is essential that the chickpeas are thoroughly cooked before blending, otherwise it will be difficult to achieve a smooth-textured hummus.

Cauliflower Pizza

1/2 tspn sugar

1/2 x 11g (1/3oz) sachet dried yeast

125ml (4fl oz) hot water

250g (8oz) plain flour, sifted

1 tblspn oil

4 tblspn tomato purée

60g (2oz) stuffed green olives

1/2 cauliflower, broken into florets, cooked

1 tblspn snipped fresh chives

8 canned anchovies, drained and sliced

125g (4oz) mozzarella cheese, grated

1 Preheat oven to 190°C (375°F, Gas 5). Combine sugar, yeast and water in a bowl, cover and stand in a warm place for 10 minutes. Place flour in a second bowl, stir in yeast mixture and oil, mix until smooth.

2 Knead dough on a lightly floured surface for 10 minutes until smooth and glossy, then place in a lightly oiled bowl, cover and stand for 30 minutes or until dough has risen.

3 Knead dough again for 3 minutes, roll out to cover a greased 28cm (11in) round pizza dish, then cover and set aside in a warm place for 15 minutes.

4 Spread pizza with tomato purée, then arrange olives, cauliflower, chives and anchovies on top and sprinkle with the cheese. Bake for 20 minutes or until cooked through.

Serves 6

Fried Aubergine Fingers

2 large aubergines

salt

125g (4oz) flour

185ml (6fl oz) milk

125g (4oz) dried breadcrumbs

oil for deep-frying

1 Cut aubergines into 5cm x 1cm (2in x 1/2in) lengths, put in colander, sprinkle with salt and set aside for 30 minutes.

Cauliflower Pizza, Fried Aubergine Fingers

2 Rinse aubergines, drain and pat dry with paper towels, then dust with flour. Dip in milk, then dredge with breadcrumbs.

3 Heat oil in a medium saucepan and fry aubergines until they are an even golden colour. Drain on paper towels, serve hot.

Serves 6-8

Red Pepper Crostini

2 large red peppers

1 French loaf, cut into 1cm (1/2in) thick slices

about 125ml (4fl oz) olive oil

4 tblspn olive pâté

375g (12oz) mozzarella cheese, cut into 5mm (1/4in) slices

salt

1 Grill red peppers until blackened all over, place in a paper bag, seal, leave to 'sweat' for 10 minutes. Remove peppers from bag, peel off skins and remove seeds and thick inner membranes. Cut flesh into 5mm (1/4in) cubes.

2 Brush one side of each bread slice with oil, place on a baking sheet oiled side down. Spread top of bread slices with olive pâté. Cover each crostini with a slice of mozzarella, cut to size if necessary, top with red pepper cubes. Sprinkle with a few drops of oil and season with salt.

3 Bake in oven for about 10 minutes until cheese melts. Serve hot.

Serves 6-8

Smoked Salmon Terrine

250g (8oz) salmon fillet, skinned

1 tblspn olive oil

1 tblspn brandy

250g (½lb) smoked salmon, roughly chopped

375ml (12fl oz) double cream

1 Slice salmon fillet into 5mm (¼in) thick slices, cut each slice into two 2.5cm x 5mm (1in x ¼in) strips.

2 Heat oil in a frying pan, add salmon strips and sauté until fish is cooked, about 3 minutes.

3 Add brandy to pan and ignite with a lighted taper. When flames have died down, remove salmon and pan juices to a plate. Allow to cool, refrigerate for about 15 minutes until barely chilled.

4 Put smoked salmon in a blender or food processor. Add 250ml (8fl oz) of the cream and pepper to taste. Purée until smooth.

5 In a large bowl combine fresh salmon strips with smoked salmon purée. Beat remaining cream until stiff, fold half thoroughly into salmon mixture to incorporate, then lightly fold in remaining cream.

6 Spoon mixture into a terrine or serving dish, cover and refrigerate overnight. Serve cold with toast or crackers.

Serves 8

Hot Spicy Cheese Rolls

2 bread rolls

60g (2oz) Cheddar cheese, grated

1 tblspn sweet fruit chutney

1 tblspn tomato sauce

½ tspn Worcestershire sauce

1 Preheat oven to 180°C (350°F, Gas 4). Cut rolls in half.

2 Mix cheese, chutney, tomato sauce and Worcestershire sauce in a bowl. Pile filling onto base of each roll. Top with other half of bread roll. Wrap rolls in foil and bake in oven for 10 minutes.

Serves 2

Artichoke Hearts Stuffed with Two Cheeses

500g (1lb) jar or can artichoke hearts, drained

60g (2oz) ricotta cheese

30g (1oz) grated Parmesan cheese

¼ red pepper, finely chopped

1 tspn finely chopped fresh parsley

¼ tspn crushed black peppercorns

1 Slice bottoms off artichoke hearts so they will stand upright.

2 Combine ricotta, Parmesan, red pepper, parsley and black pepper in a small bowl.

3 Spoon mixture into the centre of each heart and grill for 1 minute or until the cheese melts.

Serves 4

Cauliflower Gratin with Hazelnuts

1 medium cauliflower, broken into florets

1 tspn vegetable oil

1 onion, chopped

2 small cloves garlic, finely chopped

60g (2oz) hazelnuts, roughly chopped

60g (2oz) ground hazelnuts

1 tblspn soy sauce

1 tspn chopped fresh oregano

1 Preheat oven to 180°C (350°F, Gas 4). Boil, steam or microwave cauliflower until just tender. Reserve cooking liquid. Arrange florets in an ovenproof dish.

2 Heat oil in a frying pan, add onion and garlic, sauté until golden, about 5 minutes. Add chopped hazelnuts, sauté for a 4 minutes. Spoon over cauliflower.

3 Add enough water to reserved cooking liquid to make up 300ml (10fl oz). Pour into a blender or food processor, add ground hazelnuts, soy sauce and oregano. Blend, then pour over cauliflower. Bake for 20-25 minutes, or until top is golden.

Serves 4

Creamy Oyster Dip

24 oysters, removed from shells

125ml (4fl oz) double cream

60ml (2fl oz) milk

125ml (4fl oz) soured cream

2 tblspn tomato sauce

1 tspn flour

1 Rinse oysters and place in a small bowl, cover and refrigerate.

2 Combine cream, milk, soured cream, tomato sauce and flour in a small saucepan. Slowly bring to the boil over moderate heat, stirring constantly until mixture thickens. Remove from heat and stir in oysters.

Serves 4

Kipper Pâté

250g (8oz) kipper fillets

1 loaf French bread, cut into diagonal slices

1 onion, chopped

90ml (3fl oz) mayonnaise

salt

freshly ground black pepper

chopped fresh parsley for garnish

1 Place kipper fillets in a bowl, pour over boiling water to cover. Stand for 5 minutes. Meanwhile, toast bread slices.

2 Drain kippers, flake fish into clean bowl. Remove any bones. Add onion and mayonnaise, season to taste with salt and pepper. Mix well. Sprinkle top with parsley.

Serves 4

Artichoke Hearts Stuffed with Two Cheeses

Creamy Oyster Dip

FABULOUS FISH AND SEAFOOD

Succulent, full of flavour and highly nutritious, fish and seafood always make an excellent choice. On the following pages you will find recipes for all tastes and occasions, including Tuna with Sesame Seeds and Ginger, Sole Fillets with Cider Vinegar Sauce, and Red Mullet with Dill Butter.

Bream with Orange

4 medium sea bream, washed and scaled

125g (4oz) butter, melted

1 clove garlic, crushed

2 tblspn freshly squeezed lime juice

60ml (2fl oz) freshly squeezed orange juice

sliced orange and chopped fresh dill for garnish

1 Preheat oven to 180°C (350°F, Gas 4). Place each fish on a piece of foil large enough to completely enclose it. Combine melted butter, garlic, lime juice and orange juice in a small bowl and brush over fish. Wrap up in foil and bake in oven for 25 minutes.

2 Garnish with orange slices and dill. Serve with lightly cooked vegetables.

Serves 4

Kitchen Tip
Sea bream is a somewhat underrated fish and it is well worth trying this citrus-flavoured recipe. Alternatively, trout may be substituted for the sea bream. Serve this dish with steamed vegetables such as mangetout, asparagus spears, carrots and minted new potatoes.

Thai-style Mackerel

4 x 185g (6oz) mackerel fillets

juice of 1 lemon

salt

freshly ground black pepper

3 tblspn olive oil

1 onion, chopped

1 bunch fresh coriander, chopped

1/4 tspn dried crushed chillies

1 Preheat oven to 200°C (400°F, Gas 6). Make sure no bones remain in mackerel fillets. Sprinkle fish with lemon juice and season to taste with salt and pepper. Marinate at room temperature for 30 minutes.

2 Heat 1 tablespoon of the oil in a frying pan, add onion, sauté for about 5 minutes until golden. Stir in coriander and crushed chillies.

3 Use a little of remaining oil to grease an ovenproof serving dish, large enough to hold fillets in one layer. Arrange fish in dish and top with onion and coriander mixture.

4 Drizzle with remaining oil, cover with foil and bake in oven for 10 minutes, or until fish is cooked through. Serve immediately.

Serves 4

Bream with Orange

Mussels Steamed in Wine

500ml (16fl oz) dry white wine

2 large tomatoes, chopped

1 large onion, finely chopped

2 cloves garlic, finely chopped

4 tblspn finely chopped fresh parsley

60g (2oz) butter

salt

freshly ground black pepper

2kg (4lb) mussels, scrubbed and beards removed

1 Combine wine, tomatoes, onion, garlic, parsley and butter in a large saucepan. Season with salt and pepper.

2 Add mussels to pan, cover, bring to the boil, shake pan over heat for 3 minutes, or until mussels open. Remove open mussels, steam remaining mussels a little longer. Discard any mussels that do not open.

3 To serve, divide mussels between 4 deep, heated plates, ladle over liquid.

Serves 4

Tuna with Sesame Seeds and Ginger

1/2 tspn crushed black peppercorns

1 tspn salt

1 tblspn sesame seeds

2 tspn freshly grated root ginger

4 tuna steaks, 2.5cm (1in) thick

1 tblspn vegetable oil

4 spring onions, cut into 5cm (2in) diagonal slices

1 Combine black pepper, salt, sesame seeds and ginger in a small bowl, mix well. Sprinkle over tuna steaks, pat in well with your fingers.

2 Heat oil in a heavy-based frying pan, add tuna and cook until done to your liking, see Kitchen Tip. Remove fish to heated plates.

3 Add spring onions to the frying pan, sauté for about 30 seconds until they just start to soften. Spoon over fish steaks. Serve immediately.

Serves 4

Kitchen Tip
Tuna steaks do not need to be cooked to the same degree as most other fish. Some people prefer tuna cooked with only the outside seared, but still pink inside.

Sole Fillets with Cider Vinegar Sauce

30g (1oz) butter

500g (1lb) lemon sole or Dover sole fillets

Cider Vinegar Sauce

3 tblspn cider vinegar

185g (6oz) butter, cut into small pieces

salt

freshly ground black pepper

1 Melt the butter in a large frying pan, add sole fillets and cook for about 6-7 minutes until just cooked, turning once.

2 To make sauce: Bring cider vinegar to the boil over moderately high heat. Add butter, one piece at a time, to vinegar, making sure each piece has been completely incorporated before adding the next. Stir constantly, until sauce has thickened slightly, moving pan off the heat if mixture becomes too hot. Season to taste with salt and pepper. Spoon sauce over fillets and serve.

Serves 4

Crispy Fried Sardines

500g (1lb) fresh sardines

125g (4oz) flour

2 eggs, beaten

125g (4oz) dried breadcrumbs

oil for deep-frying

coriander to garnish

orange wedges and tartare sauce to serve

1 Wash and scale sardines, pat dry. Slice sardines lengthwise along the underside from head to tail, clean cavity, remove heads. Using heel of hand, press firmly along the backbone to flatten out.

2 Place the flour, beaten eggs and breadcrumbs into separate deep plates. Coat each sardine in flour, then egg and breadcrumbs. Heat the oil and deep-fry the sardines until cooked and golden. Drain on paper towels. Garnish with coriander. Serve immediately with orange wedges and tartare sauce.

Serves 4

Red Mullet Steaks with Dill Butter

3 tblspn lemon juice

1 tspn chilli paste

3 tblspn white wine

3 tblspn oil

4 red mullet steaks

Dill Butter

4 egg yolks

2 tblspn freshly squeezed lime juice

60g (2oz) butter, melted, boiling

1 tblspn chopped fresh dill

lemon slices and fresh dill sprigs for garnish

1 Combine lemon juice, chilli paste, wine and oil and brush over the red mullet. Grill fish under moderate heat for 5 minutes each side or until cooked through.

2 Make the Dill Butter: Blend egg yolks with lime juice in a blender or food processor for 1 minute. While the motor is running, add the hot butter (it is important that butter is boiling) and blend for a further 1 minute.

3 Stir in dill, pour sauce over fish and garnish with lemon slices and dill. Serve with steamed mangetout, if liked.

Serves 4

Crispy Fried Sardines, Red Mullet Steaks with Dill Butter

NOURISHING RICE, PULSES AND GRAINS

Often overlooked, rice, pulses and grains form the basis of many nourishing meals. This section includes instructions for cooking them properly, and delicious recipes such as Creamy Mushroom Risotto, Indian Lentil Dhal, and Soya Bean Casserole.

Prawn, Crab and Avocado Risotto

90g (3oz) butter

1 onion, chopped

1 clove garlic, crushed

250g (8oz) risotto rice

900ml (1¹/₂pt) hot vegetable stock

1 x 95g (3¹/₂oz) can crab meat, drained

185g (6oz) cooked, peeled prawns, thawed if frozen

1 avocado

salt

freshly ground black pepper

30g (1oz) grated Parmesan cheese

chopped fresh parsley for garnish

1 Heat 60g (2oz) of the butter in a heavy-based saucepan, add onion and garlic and sauté for 4 minutes until golden and softened.

2 Add rice to pan and cook over a gentle heat for 4 minutes, stirring constantly to coat the rice with butter.

3 Add a third of the stock to the pan, bring to the boil, then cover and simmer until the liquid has been absorbed. Gradually add more stock to the pan, cover and simmer until the stock has been absorbed. Add remaining stock, cover and simmer for about 15 minutes until the stock has been absorbed and the rice is cooked, stirring occasionally.

4 Add crab meat and prawns to pan and heat through for 5 minutes, adding a little more stock if necessary. Peel, stone and slice the avocado. Add to the pan with salt and pepper, Parmesan and remaining butter. Heat through gently and serve garnished with parsley.

Serves 4

Vegetable Stock

2 tblspn oil

2 onions, chopped

4 carrots, chopped

2 sticks celery, chopped

salt

freshly ground black pepper

2.5 litres (4pt) water

few fresh parsley sprigs

1 tspn dried thyme or 2 fresh thyme sprigs

1 bay leaf

1 clove garlic, bruised

1 Heat oil in a large saucepan and cook onions until golden. Add carrots and celery, sauté for 4 minutes, stirring. Season with salt and pepper and add 2 tablespoons of the water. Cover pan and cook over moderate heat for 5 minutes.

2 Add remaining water, bring to the boil, then skim. Add parsley, thyme, bay leaf and garlic. Reduce heat and simmer until all vegetables are tender. Strain.

Makes about 2 litres (3¹/₂pt)

Creamy Mushroom Risotto

Creamy Mushroom Risotto

30g (1oz) Chinese dried mushrooms
60g (2oz) butter
1 onion, chopped
2 cloves garlic, crushed
185g (6oz) risotto rice
250g (8oz) mushrooms, sliced
500ml (16fl oz) hot vegetable stock
3 tblspn chopped fresh parsley
30g (1oz) grated Parmesan cheese
freshly ground black pepper

1 Soak dried mushrooms in hot water for 30 minutes, drain; discard stalks, slice caps.

2 Melt butter in a saucepan, add onion and garlic, stir over heat until softened. Add rice and dried and fresh mushrooms, stir over heat for 1 minute.

3 Add 125ml (4fl oz) of vegetable stock, stir continuously until liquid has been absorbed. Keep adding vegetable stock, 125ml (4fl oz) at a time; stir continuously and allow liquid to be absorbed between additions. Mixture will become quite creamy. Stir in parsley, cheese and pepper. Serve hot.

Serves 4

Variations

If preferred, omit the Chinese dried mushrooms and add an extra 60g (2oz) fresh sliced mushrooms. Emmental, Gruyère, or mature Cheddar cheese may be substituted for the Parmesan. This risotto can be made a day ahead and kept covered in the refrigerator until required. To reheat, transfer to a saucepan, add a large knob of butter and warm through over gentle heat. Fork through and serve.

Risotto with Green Vegetables

1 tblspn sunflower oil
1 small onion, chopped
125g (4oz) risotto rice
60ml (2fl oz) dry white wine
375ml (12fl oz) water
2 tblspn chopped fresh parsley
125g (4oz) broccoli florets, blanched
125g (4oz) asparagus, blanched and chopped
125g (4oz) green peas, blanched
2 tblspn chopped fresh parsley, plus
parsley sprig for garnish

1 Heat oil in a large frying pan, add onion and cook for 3 minutes.

2 Stir in rice and wine, cook until wine is absorbed.

3 Add water, bring to the boil, cover, reduce heat and cook rice until tender and liquid is absorbed, approximately 20 minutes.

4 Stir vegetables and chopped parsley into rice and serve immediately, garnished with the parsley sprig.

Serves 4

Red Lentil and Rice Pilaf

185g (6oz) Red Lentil and Rice Pilaf Mix (recipe opposite)
750ml (1¹/₄pt) vegetable stock or water

Combine mix and vegetable stock or water in a saucepan, bring to the boil, then cover, reduce heat and simmer for about 55 minutes, or until grains are tender, adding a little extra liquid if necessary. Serve hot.

Serves 6 as an accompaniment

Risotto with Green Vegetables

Red Lentil and Rice Pilaf Mix

375g (12oz) red lentils
250g (8oz) brown rice
250g (8oz) wild rice
185g (6oz) pearl barley
125g (4oz) dried mushrooms, chopped
2 tblspn dried parsley flakes
60g (2oz) dried chopped vegetables
2 tblspn dried onion flakes
2 tblspn Italian herb seasoning
1 tblspn garlic flakes
1/2 tspn paprika
pinch of celery seed
pinch of chilli powder
pinch of dry mustard

1 Preheat oven to 150°C (300°F, Gas 2). Rinse lentils, brown and wild rice in a colander, under cold running water, drain.

2 Spread on a baking sheet, dry in oven for about 15 minutes, stirring frequently. Remove from oven, cool.

3 Place all remaining ingredients in a large bowl and mix well. Add cooled lentils and rice and stir to blend. Store in airtight containers for up to 12 months.

Makes 1.5kg (3lb)

Asparagus Risotto

125g (4oz) butter
1 small onion, sliced
500g (1lb) fresh asparagus, cut into 2,5cm (1in) pieces, set tips aside
185g (6oz) risotto rice
125ml (4fl oz) dry white wine
1 litre (1³/4pt) hot vegetable stock
2 tblspn single cream
60g (2oz) grated Parmesan cheese
salt
freshly ground black pepper

1 Melt half the butter in a saucepan, add onion and cook until golden. Add asparagus stalks, stir well. Add rice, stirring thoroughly to coat with butter. Add wine and boil over high heat until liquid has evaporated.

2 Add hot stock, a ladleful at a time, stirring constantly. Allow each ladle to be almost absorbed before adding the next. After 10 minutes, add asparagus tips, then after about 25 minutes add the cream and Parmesan. Continue stirring until well blended. Add remaining butter, a piece at a time, working in well. Season to taste with salt and pepper.

Serves 4

How to Cook Pulses (Dried beans, peas and lentils)

1 Rinse thoroughly. Remove anything that does not belong, like little pebbles or grit, etc. Drain. Rinse again.

2 Soak. There are two ways of doing this. The conventional method is to put the pulses in a bowl, cover with lots of water (for 185g [6oz] beans, use 750ml [1¹/4pt] water) and leave overnight. The alternative way is called 'the quick soak'. Put the pulses in a saucepan, cover with plenty of water, bring to the boil. Boil for 2 minutes, remove pan from heat, cover and leave for 1 hour. Drain, rinse and drain again.

3 To cook, place drained soaked pulses in a saucepan with plenty of water to cover. Do not add salt; this will toughen the skins and interfere with the pulses' cooking process. Bring the water to the boil and boil rapidly for 10 minutes. Do not skimp on this boiling time, particularly if you are cooking red kidney beans. It is necessary to destroy natural toxins. Reduce heat to a simmer and cook until beans are tender. The cooking time varies depending on the type of pulse and its age. Drain and proceed according to recipe. Season after cooking.

Note: Lentils generally do not need lengthy soaking.

Creamy Rice and Fennel

60g (2oz) butter

2 tblspn olive oil

1/2 onion, chopped

3 large fennel bulbs, chopped

1.2 litres (2pt) water

salt

500g (1lb) risotto rice

125ml (4fl oz) dry white wine

3 tblspn chopped fresh parsley

45g (1¹/₂oz) grated Parmesan cheese, plus extra to serve

1 Melt 45g (1¹/₂oz) of the butter with the olive oil over moderately high heat. Add onion, sauté for about 3 minutes until golden. Add fennel, reduce heat, cook for a further 5 minutes, until fennel begins to brown, but is still crisp. Remove from heat.

2 Bring water to the boil in a saucepan, add salt and rice, cover, reduce heat, cook until all water has been absorbed. Stir in wine and fennel mixture, cover, cook for a further 5 minutes until rice is tender. If necessary, add more water.

3 Remove from heat, stir in remaining butter, parsley and Parmesan. Serve with extra Parmesan.

Serves 6

Risotto Primavera

60ml (2fl oz) olive oil

1 onion, chopped

2 sticks celery, chopped

1 potato, peeled and cut into small cubes

1 carrot, cut into thin strips

250g (8oz) risotto rice

1 litre (1³/₄pt) vegetable stock

60g (2oz) green beans, topped and tailed, halved

125g (4oz) frozen peas, thawed

125g (4oz) yellow baby squash, sliced

6 drained canned artichoke hearts, halved

1 Heat oil in a large frying pan, add onion and celery, cook for 5 minutes. Add potato and carrot and cook for 5 minutes, stirring constantly.

2 Sprinkle the rice over the vegetables and cook for 10 minutes, stirring occasionally. Add stock, toss rice mixture and bring to the boil over moderate heat.

3 Stir in beans, peas, squash and artichokes and simmer mixture for 20 minutes, stirring constantly, until rice is cooked and the liquid absorbed.

Serves 4

Vegetable Pilaf with Almonds

2 tspn olive oil

1 onion, chopped

1 clove garlic, crushed

30g (1oz) flaked almonds

315g (10oz) long grain brown rice

1 stick celery, chopped

125g (4oz) green beans, chopped

125g (4oz) courgettes, chopped

125g (4oz) broccoli florets

1 small green pepper, chopped

30g (1oz) currants

2 tspn grated orange rind

juice of 1 orange

600ml (1pt) boiling water

1 bay leaf

1 tblspn soy sauce

1 Heat oil in a large saucepan, cook onion for 5 minutes, stirring occasionally. Add garlic, almonds and rice and cook for 2 minutes, stirring.

2 Add vegetables, currants, orange rind, orange juice, boiling water and bay leaf. Bring to the boil, then cover, reduce heat and simmer for 30 minutes or until rice is cooked. Add soy sauce and cook covered for a further 5 minutes. Remove bay leaf before serving.

Serves 4

Vegetable Pilaf with Almonds

Indian Lentil Dhal

Indian Lentil Dhal

250g (8oz) lentils
375ml (12fl oz) water
1 onion, chopped
1/4 tspn turmeric
2 tspn chopped fresh coriander
1 green chilli, chopped
1 x 440g (14oz) can chopped tomatoes
parsley sprig for garnish

1 Rinse lentils under cold running water until water runs clear, drain. Place lentils in a saucepan with measured water and onion, bring to the boil, cover, reduce heat and simmer for 15 minutes or until lentils are tender; spoon off froth occasionally during cooking. Mash lentils and any remaining cooking liquid with a fork until smooth.

2 Stir in turmeric, coriander, chilli and tomatoes with the can juices. Cover, bring to the boil, then reduce heat and simmer for 10 minutes or until mixture has thickened. Spoon into a serving dish and serve at room temperature, garnished with parsley. Serve with naan bread.

Serves 4

Spinach and Rice Balls with Tomato Sauce

Spinach and Rice Balls with Tomato Sauce

| 12 spinach leaves, chopped finely |
| 90g (3oz) cooked rice |
| 1/2 tspn grated nutmeg |
| 30g (1oz) grated Parmesan cheese |
| 2 tblspn grated lemon rind |
| 125g (4oz) Cheddar cheese, grated |
| 3 eggs |
| 125g (4oz) fresh breadcrumbs |
| oil for deep frying |

Tomato Sauce

| 15g (1/2oz) butter |
| 1 onion, chopped |
| 1 x 440g (14oz) can chopped tomatoes |
| 2 tblspn chopped fresh basil |

1 Steam spinach in a little water until wilted; drain and squeeze out excess liquid. Combine spinach, rice, nutmeg, Parmesan cheese, lemon rind, cheese and 2 of the eggs. Mix well. Reserve remaining egg, lightly beaten, in a shallow dish. Spread out breadcrumbs on a baking sheet.

2 Roll heaped tablespoons of mixture into balls, dip in egg, then roll in breadcrumbs, refrigerate 30 minutes.

3 For the sauce, melt butter in a saucepan, add onion, stir over heat until tender. Add tomatoes with the can juices, cover and simmer for 10 minutes or until reduced and thickened. Stir in basil.

4 Deep fry spinach and rice balls in hot oil until golden brown, then drain on kitchen paper. Serve hot with tomato sauce.

Makes 16

Kitchen Tip
This recipe makes a good dish for midweek entertaining as it may be prepared in advance. Prepare the rice balls up to the end of step 2, and make the sauce. To serve, simply deep fry spinach and rice balls, and reheat sauce.

Lentil Burgers

90g (3oz) cooked lentils

250g (8oz) cooked potato, mashed

1 onion, finely chopped

45g (1¹/₂oz) rolled oats

15g (¹/₂oz) fresh wholemeal breadcrumbs

2 tspn desiccated coconut

1 tspn ground cumin

large pinch chilli powder

2 egg whites, beaten

2 tblspn chopped fresh parsley

2 tblspn freshly squeezed lime juice

155g (5oz) oat bran

olive oil

1 Combine all ingredients, except oat bran and oil in bowl. Form mixture into 4 patties. Coat in oat bran.

2 Brush both sides of patties with oil. Cook under grill until heated through and golden on both sides. Serve with salad.

Serves 4

Lentils with Baked Eggs

185g (6oz) Continental lentils

1 tblspn oil

1 onion, finely chopped

1 carrot, chopped

125g (4oz) mushrooms, sliced

1 stick celery, chopped

2 cloves garlic, crushed

1 litre (1³/₄pt) water

4 eggs

1 tblspn chopped fresh parsley

1 Preheat oven to 200°C (400°F, Gas 6). Soak lentils for several hours in plenty of water. Drain then rinse and drain again. Set aside.

2 Heat oil in a flameproof saucepan for 2-3 minutes, add onion, carrot, mushrooms and celery and cook until vegetables have softened. Add garlic and mix well.

3 Stir in lentils and add water. Bring to the boil, then reduce heat and simmer for about 45 minutes until lentils are tender.

4 Put lentils in a buttered ovenproof baking dish, make 4 indentations in the mixture, break in eggs. Bake in oven for about 20 minutes until eggs are cooked. Sprinkle with parsley and serve immediately.

Serves 4

Cottage Pie with Lentils and Vegetables

220g (7oz) red lentils, washed

2 bay leaves

500g (1lb) assorted chopped vegetables, such as carrots, Brussels sprouts, courgettes, cauliflower, broccoli, beans, pumpkin, parsnip, celery or cabbage

salt

6 potatoes, cooked, drained and mashed with milk

2 tspn sesame seeds

1/4 tspn paprika

Sauce

1 tspn olive oil

1 onion, finely chopped

1 clove garlic, crushed

3 tblspn tomato purée

1 1/2 tblspn cornflour mixed with 2 tblspn water

2 tblspn chopped fresh parsley

1 Combine lentils and bay leaves in a saucepan, add water to cover, bring to the boil, then cover and simmer for 15 minutes. Drain, reserving 500ml (16fl oz) stock for sauce. Discard bay leaves. Spread lentils over base of a 2 litre (3 1/2pt) ovenproof dish.

2 Cook vegetables in boiling salted water for 5 minutes or until just tender. Drain and place on top of lentils.

3 To make sauce, heat oil in a saucepan, cook onion for 5 minutes, stirring occasionally. Add garlic, reserved lentil stock and tomato purée. Bring sauce to the boil, then stir in cornflour mixture and parsley. Return sauce to the boil and cook, stirring, for 5 minutes until sauce boils and thickens.

4 Spoon sauce over vegetables. Spoon or pipe mashed potatoes over vegetables; sprinkle with sesame seeds and paprika. Bake in oven for 40 minutes.

Serves 4

Soya Bean Casserole

1 tblspn olive oil

1/2 tspn chilli powder

1 tspn grated fresh root ginger

1 clove garlic, crushed

4 spring onions, chopped

125g (4oz) mushrooms, sliced

2 sticks celery, chopped

2 carrots, chopped

1 x 225g (7oz) can water chestnuts, drained and sliced

1 tblspn cornflour

1 tblspn sherry

1 tblspn honey

1 tblspn soy sauce

250ml (8fl oz) vegetable stock

310g (10oz) cooked soya beans, drained (see page 25)

1 Heat oil in a saucepan, add chilli, ginger and garlic, cook for 1 minute. Add vegetables, including water chestnuts, cover and cook for 10 minutes.

2 Combine cornflour, sherry, honey, soy sauce and stock. Mix well and add to vegetables with soya beans. Stir until sauce boils and thickens, reduce heat, cover and simmer for 10 minutes. Serve.

Serves 4

Cottage Pie with Lentils and Vegetables

Lentil and Vegetable Pockets

250g (8oz) red lentils, washed

15g (1/2oz) butter

1 onion, chopped

2 cloves garlic, crushed

2 carrots, chopped

1 tomato, chopped

1 tblspn chopped fresh oregano

125ml (4fl oz) water

12 spinach leaves, chopped

1 tblspn lemon juice

6 pitta breads

1 Cook lentils in a saucepan of boiling water for 30 minutes or until tender. Drain.

2 Heat butter in a pan, add onion and garlic, stir over heat until onion has softened. Add carrots, tomato, oregano and water, bring to the boil, then simmer until carrots are tender.

3 Add spinach, lemon juice and lentils, simmer until reduced and thickened.

4 Warm pitta breads under a low grill for 2-3 minutes. Cut in half, spoon hot lentil mixture into pockets and serve immediately.

Serves 6

White Beans in Tomato Sauce

185g (6oz) dried white haricot beans

1 onion, chopped

2 tblspn oil

6 tomatoes, peeled, seeded and chopped

1 clove garlic, crushed

salt

freshly ground black pepper

2 tspn finely chopped fresh parsley

1 Soak and cook beans according to instructions on page 25. They will require about 1 1/2 hours. Drain.

Lentil and Vegetable Pockets

2 Heat oil in saucepan over moderate heat, cook onions until golden. Add tomatoes, garlic, and salt and pepper and cook until very little liquid is left. Stir in parsley. Add cooked beans and heat through.

Serves 4

Courgette and Butterbean Bake

500g (1lb) dried butterbeans

3 tblspn olive oil

750g (1 1/2lb) courgettes, sliced

1 onion, chopped

1 green chilli, chopped

1 clove garlic, crushed

375ml (12fl oz) tomato sauce, for recipe see page 29

1 tblspn chilli powder, optional

2 tblspn chopped fresh coriander

salt

125g (4oz) Cheddar cheese, grated

1 Soak and cook beans according to instructions on page 25. They will require about 1 1/4 hours. Drain, reserving 185ml (6fl oz) of the cooking liquid. Preheat oven to 180°C (350°F, Gas 4).

2 Heat 2 tablespoons olive oil in saucepan, sauté courgettes. Remove to plate, set aside.

3 Add remaining oil to pan, sauté onion, chilli and garlic until onion is soft and golden. Add tomato sauce, cooked beans and reserved liquid, chilli powder if using, coriander and salt to taste. Bring to the boil, reduce heat and simmer for 10 minutes.

4 Place a third of the courgette slices in a large ovenproof casserole, pour over a third of the bean mixture, then top with 25g (1oz) of Cheddar. Repeat layers.

5 Add remaining courgettes and top with bean mixture. Cover and bake for 30 minutes. Sprinkle with remaining cheese and cook until cheese melts.

Serves 6

Bean Curry

1 onion, roughly chopped

5cm (2in) piece fresh root ginger, peeled and chopped

2 cloves garlic, peeled

1 tblspn olive oil

2 tspn curry powder

1 tspn ground cumin

1 tspn turmeric

60g (2oz) sweet fruit chutney

90g (3oz) crunchy peanut butter

1 x 440g (14oz) can chopped tomatoes

2 tblspn tomato purée

250ml (8fl oz) water

1 x 310g (10oz) can butter beans, drained

1 x 310g (10oz) can red kidney beans, drained

1 Puree onion, ginger and garlic in a blender or food processor.

2 Heat oil in saucepan, cook onion mixture for 5 minutes, stirring occasionally. Add curry powder, cumin and turmeric and cook for 1 minute, stirring.

3 Add chutney, peanut butter, tomatoes with can juices, tomato purée, water and beans. Stir until well combined. Bring to the boil, then cover and simmer for 20 minutes. Serve with rice.

Serves 4

Peppery Red Kidney Beans

375g (12oz) dried red kidney beans, soaked

2 onions, finely chopped

2 cloves garlic, crushed

2 fresh green chillies, chopped

1 bay leaf

2 tblspn oil

salt

1 large tomato, peeled and chopped

1 Rinse and drain kidney beans and place in saucepan with water to cover. Add 1 onion, 1 clove garlic, chillies and bay leaf.

2 Bring to the boil and boil hard for 10 minutes. Reduce heat and simmer until beans are tender, adding more water as required. Start checking after 1 hour, but they could take longer; do not overcook. Add salt to taste. Discard bay leaf.

3 Cook remaining onion in oil in a frying pan until softened. Add remaining garlic and tomato and cook until mixture thickens.

4 Measure 185g (6oz) of the beans, add to tomato mixture with a little of the cooking liquid and mash until smooth. Stir into remaining beans in pan and heat through for a few minutes. Serve hot.

Serves 6

Barley and Vegetable Curry

60g (2oz) butter

4 leeks, sliced (white part only)

2 cloves garlic, crushed

2 tspn curry powder

1/2 tspn garam masala

375g (12oz) pearl barley, rinsed and drained

2 large potatoes, peeled and cut into 2cm (3/4in) cubes

375g (12oz) pumpkin, cut into 2cm (3/4in) cubes

1 litre (1 3/4pt) water

250g (8oz) broccoli, broken into florets

1 Melt butter in large saucepan, add leeks, stir over heat until tender. Add garlic, curry powder and garam masala, stir over heat for 1 minute.

2 Add pearl barley, potatoes, pumpkin and water, cover and bring to the boil, then simmer for 10 minutes. Add broccoli and simmer for a further 10 minutes or until vegetables and barley are tender.

Serves 4

Barley and Vegetable Curry

Curried Vegetables with Almonds

4 tblspn oil

2 cloves garlic, crushed

1/4 tspn cayenne

1 tblspn ground coriander

1 tspn ground cumin

2 tspn turmeric

2.5cm (1in) piece fresh root ginger, peeled and thinly sliced

2 sticks celery, sliced

2 leeks, sliced

2 potatoes, cut into 2cm (3/4in) cubes

2 aubergines, unpeeled, cut into 2cm (3/4in) cubes

1 fresh green chilli, chopped

1 small cauliflower, broken into florets

250ml (8fl oz) canned coconut cream, see Kitchen Tip

500g (1lb) tomatoes, peeled, seeded and chopped

125g (4oz) blanched almonds

250g (8oz) basmati rice

salt

1 Heat oil in a saucepan and sauté garlic and spices for 4 minutes. Add celery, leeks, potatoes, aubergines and chilli, combine well and cook for 4 minutes. Add cauliflower and cook for a further 4 minutes, stirring constantly.

2 Stir in coconut cream and tomatoes, cover and cook for 20 minutes or until all vegetables are tender. Add almonds, keep warm.

3 Cook rice in very lightly salted boiling water until tender. Serve on heated plates topped with curried vegetables.

Serves 6

Kitchen Tip
Coconut cream may be replaced with 90g (3oz) creamed coconut dissolved in 250ml (8fl oz) warm water.

Pearl Barley with Vegetables

30g (1oz) butter

1 small onion, chopped

2 sticks celery, chopped

90g (3oz) mushrooms, chopped

185g (6oz) pearl barley

500ml (16fl oz) vegetable stock

salt

1 Melt butter in a saucepan and sauté onion and celery for about 5 minutes until onion is golden. Add mushrooms and sauté for a further 3 minutes.

2 Add barley. Mix well. Add half the vegetable stock, season to taste with salt, bring to the boil, then cover and simmer for 25 minutes.

3 Add remaining stock and simmer for a further 25 minutes, until all the liquid has been absorbed. Fluff up barley with a fork. Serve hot.

Serves 6

Pearl Barley and Potato Casserole

1kg (2lb) potatoes

155g (5oz) pearl barley

salt

freshly ground black pepper

2 tblspn chopped fresh dill

440ml (14fl oz) milk

30g (1oz) butter, melted

1 Preheat oven to 180°C (350°F, Gas 4). Cook potatoes in a saucepan of lightly salted boiling water until just tender. When cool enough to handle, peel potatoes and cut into 5mm (1/4in) slices.

2 Rinse barley thoroughly under cold running water; drain. Place in a pan with water to cover and a pinch of salt, bring to the boil, then simmer for 10 minutes; drain.

3 Grease an ovenproof serving dish. Place half the potatoes in the dish, and season with salt and pepper. Cover with the barley, sprinkle with dill.

4 Top with remaining potato slices, season with salt and pepper. Pour over milk and brush top potato layer generously with butter.

5 Bake in oven for 1 hour or until potatoes are cooked and golden. Serve hot.

Serves 4

Pilau with Apricots and Sultanas

15g (1/2oz) butter

15g (1/2oz) flaked almonds

1 clove garlic, crushed

1/2 small onion, chopped

1/2 tspn grated fresh root ginger

1/2 tspn salt

1 clove

2.5cm (1in) cinnamon stick

1/2 tspn turmeric

125g (4oz) long grain rice

470ml (15fl oz) water

30g (1oz) dried apricots, chopped

1 tblspn sultanas

1 Melt butter in a flameproof casserole, add almonds and sauté until golden. Add garlic, onion and ginger and sauté for about 5 minutes, until onion is golden.

2 Stir in salt, clove, cinnamon, turmeric and rice.

3 Add water, bring to the boil, then cover and simmer for about 25 minutes, or until all the water has been absorbed.

4 Stir in apricots and sultanas and fluff up rice with a fork. Serve hot.

Serves 6 as an accompaniment

Barley and Tomato Casserole with Olives

Barley and Tomato Casserole with Olives

185g (6oz) pearl barley
250ml (8fl oz) water
2 tblspn sunflower oil
375g (12oz) tomatoes, peeled, seeded and chopped
60ml (2fl oz) dry white wine
3 tblspn tomato purée
1 large onion, chopped
60g (2oz) stuffed green olives, halved
oregano sprig for garnish

1 Soak barley in water for 2 hours, drain well.

2 Heat oil in a large frying pan over moderate heat. Add barley and cook for 10 minutes, stirring constantly.

3 Add the tomatoes, wine and tomato purée and simmer for 20 minutes.

4 Add onion and cook for a further 5 minutes. Stir in olives and serve immediately garnished with oregano.

Serves 8

Variation

Pearl barley is a refined form of barley which has been polished to remove the bran. Although it is a source of Vitamin B, its nutritional value is less than pot barley. Try it as a change from rice, pasta or potatoes, or enjoy it in dishes such as this one.

Buckwheat Noodles with Julienne Vegetables

125g (4oz) green beans

1 small red pepper

125g (4oz) mangetout

1 carrot

1 tblspn olive oil

1 clove garlic, crushed

1 tspn grated fresh root ginger

1 tspn sesame oil

1 tblspn soy sauce

1 x 225g (7oz) can water chestnuts, drained and sliced

250g (8oz) buckwheat noodles

1 tblspn olive oil

1 tblspn chopped fresh coriander for garnish

1 Cut beans, red pepper, mangetout and carrot into thin strips.

2 Heat oil in large frying pan or wok, stir-fry vegetables and garlic for 3 minutes. Add ginger, sesame oil, soy sauce and water chestnuts, cook until heated through.

3 Cook buckwheat noodles in large saucepan of boiling water for 5 minutes or until tender; drain.

4 Divide noodles between 4 heated plates and top with vegetable mixture. Serve garnished with coriander.

Serves 4

Barley Casserole

2 tblspn olive oil

125g (4oz) small mushrooms, quartered

1 stick celery, chopped

1 carrot, chopped

1 onion, chopped

1 clove garlic, crushed

125g (4oz) pearl barley

600ml (1pt) boiling vegetable stock

2 tblspn chopped fresh parsley for garnish

1 Preheat oven to 180°C (350°F, Gas 4). Heat half the oil in saucepan and sauté mushrooms, celery, carrot, onion and garlic for 5 minutes, stirring occasionally. Remove from pan.

2 Heat remaining oil in pan, cook barley until golden, stirring continually.

3 Combine the barley and vegetables in an ovenproof casserole, add boiling stock, then cover and bake in oven for 1 hour. Serve garnished with parsley.

Serves 4

Tacos with Bean Filling

12 taco shells

1 avocado, peeled, stoned and sliced

2 tblspn lemon juice

90g (3oz) cottage cheese

1/4 Iceberg lettuce, finely shredded

1 tomato, finely chopped

1 tblspn chilli sauce, optional

Bean Filling

1 onion, finely chopped

2 tspn olive oil

45g (1 1/2oz) packet taco seasoning

1/4 tspn chilli powder

1 red pepper, finely chopped

1 courgette, finely chopped

1 x 310g (10oz) can red kidney beans, drained

1 x 440g (14oz) can chopped tomatoes

2 tblspn tomato purée

1 Preheat oven to 180°C (350°F, Gas 4). Place taco shells on a baking sheet and bake in oven for 5 minutes. Alternatively, warm taco shells under a moderate grill for 3-4 minutes.

2 Make bean filling by frying onion in oil until soft, then stirring in remaining ingredients. Cook, stirring, for 5 minutes.

3 Use bean filling to half fill taco shells. Brush avocado slices with lemon juice. Divide cottage cheese between taco shells, then top each with shredded lettuce, tomato, chilli sauce if using and avocado slices. Serve immediately.

Serves 6

Falafel

1 x 410g (13oz) can chickpeas, drained

1 onion, quartered

2 cloves garlic, chopped

125g (4oz) fresh white breadcrumbs

1/4 tspn cumin seeds

4 small dried red chillies, crushed

1 tblspn chopped fresh parsley

salt

freshly ground black pepper

1 egg, beaten

45g (1 1/2oz) dried golden breadcrumbs

vegetable oil for deep frying

4 pitta breads, warmed

shredded lettuce, sliced onion and sliced tomato to serve

1 Put the chickpeas, onion, garlic, breadcrumbs, cumin seeds and chillies in a blender or food processor. Blend ingredients until smooth, then turn mixture into a bowl, add parsley, salt and pepper and egg and mix well.

2 Form mixture into 8 balls and coat in dried breadcrumbs. Flatten each ball slightly to form oval shapes.

3 Half-fill a deep fat pan or fryer with oil. Heat to 190°C (375°F) or until a cube of day-old bread browns in 40 seconds. Fry the falafel, a few at a time, for 3 minutes until golden brown. Drain on paper towels.

4 Cut each pitta bread in half and open out to form pockets. Put a falafel in each pocket with a little shredded lettuce, a few onion slices and tomato. Serve immediately.

Serves 4

Tacos with Bean Filling

Penne with Chickpeas and Cauliflower

250g (8oz) dried chickpeas

2 cloves garlic, roughly chopped

3 tblspn olive oil

1 red chilli, seeded and finely chopped

1/2 cauliflower, broken into florets

375g (12oz) tomatoes, peeled, seeded and chopped

1 tblspn chopped fresh basil

1 tblspn red wine vinegar

30g (1oz) green olives, sliced

3 tblspn chopped fresh parsley

500g (1lb) penne

grated Parmesan cheese

1 Cook chickpeas according to instructions on page 25. Drain.

2 Sauté the garlic in olive oil until golden. Add chilli and cauliflower and cook for 3 minutes, stirring constantly.

3 Add tomatoes, basil, vinegar and olive slices, bring to the boil, then simmer until cauliflower is tender. Add chickpeas and parsley, heat through.

4 Cook penne in salted boiling water until *al dente* (see page 42). Drain. Place half the sauce in a heated serving bowl, add drained pasta, toss and top with remaining sauce. Serve hot with Parmesan.

Serves 6

Kitchen Tip
Couscous is made by steaming, drying and cracking the grain of durum wheat. From the Mediterranean countries of North Africa, it makes a delicious addition to vegetable casseroles, and is a good base for pilaf and salad dishes.

Couscous with Cauliflower, Onions and Red Pepper

375ml (12fl oz) water

2 tblspn olive oil

1/2 tspn salt

185g (6oz) couscous

1 small cauliflower, broken into florets

1 onion, thinly sliced

1 red pepper, cut into 2cm (3/4in) squares

12 black olives, stoned and chopped

salt

freshly ground black pepper

Dressing

2 tspn Dijon mustard

1 tblspn red wine vinegar

2 tspn chopped fresh thyme, or 1/2 tspn dried

75ml (2 1/2fl oz) olive oil

1 To make dressing: Combine mustard, vinegar, thyme and oil in a screwtop jar, shake until well combined. Set aside.

2 Bring water and oil to the boil in a small saucepan, stir in salt and couscous and immediately remove pan from heat. Cover and set aside.

3 Spoon 60ml (2fl oz) of the dressing into a large bowl, add cauliflower, onion and red pepper and toss well to coat. Heat a frying pan over moderately high heat, add vegetables and sauté for about 8 minutes until vegetables are tender and golden.

4 Return vegetables to the bowl. Add remaining dressing and olives and season to taste with salt and pepper. Toss thoroughly.

5 Divide couscous between 4 plates, top with the vegetables, and serve.

Serves 4

Risi e Bisi

60g (2oz) butter

1 onion, sliced

1 medium aubergine, cut into strips

1 red pepper, cut into thin strips

250g (8oz) basmati rice

1 litre (1 3/4pt) vegetable stock

2 tblspn chopped fresh parsley

1 tspn crushed black peppercorns

60g (2oz) grated Parmesan cheese

1 Melt the butter in a large frying pan over moderate heat. Add the onion, aubergine and red pepper and sauté for 2 minutes, remove with a slotted spoon.

2 Add rice to the pan, pour in the stock, cover and cook for 15 minutes, stirring occasionally until rice is cooked and about 250ml (8fl oz) of stock remains.

3 Stir in vegetables, parsley, crushed peppercorns and Parmesan. Transfer to serving dish.

Serves 4

Couscous Pilaf

155g (5oz) butter

1 onion, finely chopped

1 large carrot, chopped

200g (6 1/2oz) couscous

200g (6 1/2oz) frozen peas, thawed

75g (2 1/2oz) blanched almonds, toasted

250ml (8fl oz) vegetable stock

chopped fresh parsley to garnish

1 Melt 45g (1 1/2oz) of the butter in a large, deep frying pan over moderate heat. Add the onion and carrot and cook for 3 minutes.

2 Add the couscous, peas, almonds and stock to the pan, gently simmer mixture for 5 minutes, blend with a fork.

3 Cut remaining butter into small cubes, sprinkle over the mixture and fluff up with a fork. Serve warm, with parsley.

Serves 4

Risi e Bisi, Couscous Pilaf

PLENTIFUL PASTA

Quick to cook and satisfying, pasta always makes a welcome meal. Combine it with a rich tomato and aubergine sauce in Ratatouille Lasagne, with olives and cauliflower in Spinach Fusilli with Sautéed Cauliflower and Feta, or with salmon and Parmesan cheese in Tagliatelle with Salmon and Cream Sauce. For best results, cook the pasta until it is tender but still retains a 'bite'. The Italian term, now accepted worldwide, is al dente.

Ratatouille Lasagne

1 small aubergine, thinly sliced
salt
2 tspn olive oil
1 onion, finely chopped
1 clove garlic, crushed
1 red pepper, chopped
2 courgettes, chopped
1 x 440g (14oz) can chopped tomatoes
3 tblspn tomato purée
1/2 tspn dried basil
1/2 tspn dried oregano
8 sheets no-precook lasagne
90g (3oz) cottage cheese
1 tblspn grated Parmesan cheese
125g (4oz) mozzarella cheese, cut into strips
chopped fresh parsley for garnish

1 Preheat oven to 180°C (350°F, Gas 4). Spread aubergine slices out on wire rack, sprinkle with salt on both sides, stand for 15 minutes, then rinse and pat dry with paper towels.

2 Heat oil in saucepan and cook onion for 5 minutes, stirring occasionally. Add aubergine, garlic, red pepper, courgettes, tomatoes with can juices, tomato purée, basil and oregano. Cook for 20 minutes, stirring occasionally.

3 Spread a quarter of the aubergine mixture over the base of 20cm (8in) square or 23cm (9in) round ovenproof dish, place 4 lasagne sheets on top, then add another quarter of the aubergine mixture, then half the cottage cheese.

4 Repeat with another quarter of aubergine mixture, 4 more sheets of lasagne, remaining aubergine mixture and cottage cheese. Top with Parmesan and mozzarella. Bake in oven for 35 minutes until bubbling hot and golden. Serve garnished with parsley.

Serves 4

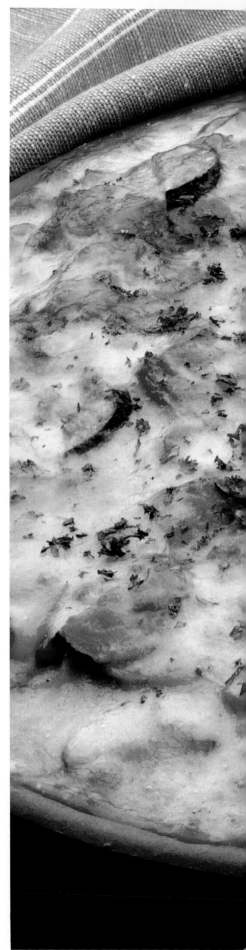

Ratatouille Lasagne

Spaghetti with Anchovy Wine Sauce

1 tblspn olive oil

1 onion, chopped

1 tspn finely chopped garlic

8 canned anchovies, drained and chopped

125ml (4fl oz) white wine

250ml (8fl oz) water

freshly ground black pepper

3 tblspn finely chopped fresh parsley

500g (1lb) spaghetti, cooked

grated Parmesan cheese

1 Heat oil in saucepan, add onion and garlic and cook until onion is softened and golden. Add anchovies and wine. Bring to the boil and cook until wine has reduced to a third.

2 Add water and bring back to the boil. Cook until sauce has thickened slightly; season with pepper. Keep warm. Stir parsley into sauce, pour over hot spaghetti and serve with Parmesan.

Serves 6

Elbow Macaroni with Danish Blue Cheese

250ml (8fl oz) double cream

185g (6oz) Danish Blue cheese, cut into cubes

500g (1lb) elbow macaroni, cooked

3 tblspn grated Parmesan cheese

1 Combine cream and cheese in a saucepan. Bring to the boil over moderate heat, stirring constantly. Allow to boil for 30 seconds only, remove from heat and set aside.

2 Spoon sauce over hot pasta, add Parmesan cheese. Toss thoroughly to coat and season with pepper. Serve immediately.

Serves 4

Spaghetti with Sweetcorn and Coriander Sauce

1 egg

2 tomatoes, peeled, seeded and chopped

1 tblspn red wine vinegar

185g (6oz) cooked sweetcorn kernels

250g (8oz) spaghetti, cooked

4 tblspn chopped fresh coriander

coriander sprig for garnish

1 In a blender or food processor, blend egg until light and fluffy, add half of the chopped tomatoes and the vinegar and blend for a further 1 minute.

2 Add sweetcorn and tomato and egg mixture to hot spaghetti, then add chopped coriander and remaining tomato and toss well to coat. Serve at once, garnished with coriander.

Serves 4

Penne with Chilli and Vodka Tomato Sauce

155ml (5fl oz) vodka

1/4 tspn dried crushed chillies

1 x 440g (14oz) can tomatoes, drained and puréed

250ml (8fl oz) double cream

salt

500g (1lb) penne, cooked

4 tblspn grated Parmesan cheese

1 Combine vodka and crushed chillies in a heavy-based saucepan, simmer over moderate heat for 2 minutes. Add puréed tomatoes and cream. Simmer for a further 5 minutes. Season with salt. Keep warm.

2 Pour sauce over hot pasta and mix thoroughly. Stir in Parmesan and serve immediately.

Serves 4

Spaghetti with Sweetcorn and Coriander Sauce

Pasta Shells with Anchovy and Onion Sauce

60ml (2fl oz) olive oil
3 onions, chopped
1 clove garlic, crushed
125ml (4fl oz) dry white wine
8 canned anchovies, drained
1 tspn chopped fresh rosemary
250ml (8fl oz) vegetable stock
1/2 fresh chilli, seeded and cut into rings
500g (1lb) small pasta shells, cooked
grated Parmesan cheese to serve

1 Heat the oil in a large frying pan, add the onions and garlic and cook until tender. Add the wine and anchovies and boil for about 2 minutes until the wine has evaporated.

2 Add the rosemary and the stock and boil until sauce is slightly thickened.

3 Spoon sauce over hot pasta shells, add chilli and toss to combine. Serve with Parmesan.

Serves 4

Wholewheat Pasta with Chunky Tomato Sauce

2 tblspn olive oil
1 onion, chopped
1 clove garlic, crushed
1 x 440g (14oz) can chopped tomatoes
60ml (2fl oz) dry white wine
1 tblspn chopped fresh basil
salt
freshly ground black pepper
500g (1lb) wholewheat penne, cooked

1 Heat the oil in a medium frying pan, add the onion and cook until tender, about 4 minutes.

2 Stir in the garlic, add the tomatoes and wine and cook over moderate heat, stirring constantly, breaking up the chopped tomatoes with the side of

the spoon. Add basil, salt and pepper and simmer sauce, uncovered, until slightly thickened.

3 Mix hot pasta in sauce and serve immediately.

Serves 4

Spinach Fusilli with Sautéed Cauliflower and Feta

200g (6¹/₂oz) green olives

1 red pepper, cut into strips

250g (8oz) feta cheese, crumbled

1 tspn freshly grated lemon rind

1 small onion, finely chopped

1 tblspn lemon juice

125ml (4fl oz) olive oil

1 cauliflower, broken into florets

625g (1¹/₄lb) spinach fusilli or small pasta shells, cooked

1 Combine olives, red pepper, feta, lemon rind, onion, lemon juice and 2 tablespoons of the olive oil in a large bowl.

2 Heat remaining oil in a heavy-based frying pan and sauté cauliflower for about 4 minutes until crisp and golden.

3 Add cauliflower and hot fusilli to remaining ingredients in bowl. Toss well. Season to taste with salt and pepper. Serve hot.

Serves 6

Pasta Shells with Spinach Cream Sauce

¹/₂ onion, finely chopped

2 tblspn olive oil

60ml (2fl oz) milk

2kg (4lb) spinach, stems removed and leaves roughly chopped

60ml (2fl oz) double cream

500g (1lb) large pasta shells, cooked

Pasta Shells with Anchovy and Onion Sauce, Wholewheat Pasta with Chunky Tomato Sauce

1 Sauté onion in half the oil in a large flameproof casserole for about 5 minutes until golden.

2 Add milk and spinach to the casserole, cover and steam for about 3 minutes over a moderately low heat until spinach is wilting. Stir spinach to ensure even cooking, then cook for a further 7 minutes. Remove lid, cook over moderate heat for about 3 minutes until liquid is reduced by half.

3 Add cream and remaining oil to casserole, season with salt and pepper. Keep warm.

4 Add hot pasta to spinach and cream mixture, toss well over moderate heat to heat through. Serve immediately.

Serves 6

Tagliatelle with Salmon and Cream Sauce

60g (2oz) butter

750ml (1¹/₄pt) double cream

60g (2oz) grated Parmesan cheese

500g (1lb) cooked salmon fillet, skinned and flaked

2 tblspn chopped fresh dill

salt

freshly ground black pepper

a pinch of grated nutmeg

375g (12oz) mixed green and white tagliatelle, cooked

dill sprigs for garnish

1 Melt the butter with the cream in a large saucepan over gentle heat. Bring to just below boiling point, then simmer for a further 10 minutes until thickened and slightly reduced. Stir in Parmesan.

2 Stir salmon, chopped dill, salt, pepper and nutmeg into cream sauce and heat through gently. Spoon sauce over hot tagliatelle, garnish with dill.

Serves 4

Index

Adzuki Bean and Pasta Soup	4
Artichoke Hearts Stuffed with Two Cheeses	16
Asparagus Risotto	25
Asparagus Soup	9
Avocado Soup	8
Barley and Tomato Casserole with Olives	37
Barley and Vegetable Curry	34
Barley Casserole	38
Bean Curry	34
Beetroot Soup	8
Beetroot Timbales with Mustard Dill Sauce	14
Bream with Orange	18
Buckwheat Noodles with Julienne Vegetables	38
Cauliflower Gratin with Hazelnuts	16
Cauliflower Pizza	15
Cold Cucumber Soup	8
Cottage Pie with Lentils and Vegetables	31
Courgette and Butterbean Bake	33
Courgette Soup with Curry Puffs	7
Couscous Pilaf	40
Couscous with Cauliflower, Onions and Red Pepper	40
Creamy Mushroom Risotto	23
Creamy Oyster Dip	17
Creamy Rice and Fennel	26
Crispy Fried Sardines	20
Crunchy Chickpeas	14
Curried Vegetables with Almonds	35
Dill Dip	13
Elbow Macaroni with Danish Blue Cheese	44
Falafel	39
French Onion Soup	4
Fresh Pea Soup with Radishes	4
Fried Aubergine Fingers	15
Gazpacho	8
Golden Fried Mozzarella	10
Guacamole	12
Hot Spicy Cheese Rolls	16
How to Cook Pulses	25
Hummus	14
Indian Lentil Dhal	28
Jerusalem Artichoke Soup	3
Kipper Pâté	17
Lentil and Vegetable Pockets	33
Lentil Burgers	30
Lentil Soup	3
Lentils with Baked Eggs	30
Mussels Steamed in Wine	20
Onion Soufflé	11
Parsnip and Coriander Soup	3
Pasta Shells with Anchovy and Onion Sauce	46
Pasta Shells with Spinach Cream Sauce	47
Pearl Barley and Potato Casserole	36
Pearl Barley with Vegetables	36
Penne with Chickpeas and Cauliflower	40
Penne with Chilli and Vodka Tomato Sauce	44
Peppery Red Kidney Beans	34
Pilau with Apricots and Sultanas	36
Pimiento and Tomato Soup	2
Prawn, Crab and Avocado Risotto	22
Prawn Mousse	14
Pumpkin Soup	7
Ratatouille Lasagne	42
Red Lentil and Rice Pilaf	24
Red Lentil and Rice Pilaf Mix	25
Red Mullet with Dill Butter	20
Red Pepper Crostini	15
Risi e Bisi	40
Risotto Primavera	26
Risotto with Green Vegetables	24
Smoked Salmon Terrine	16
Smoked Salmon Pâté	12
Sole Fillets with Cider Vinegar Sauce	20
Soya Bean Casserole	31
Spaghetti with Anchovy Wine Sauce	44
Spaghetti with Sweetcorn and Coriander Sauce	44
Spinach and Feta Filo Logs	10
Spinach and Rice Balls with Tomato Sauce	29
Spinach Fusilli with Sautéed Cauliflower and Feta	47
Sweet Potato Vichyssoise	6
Tacos with Bean Filling	39
Tagliatelle with Salmon and Cream Sauce	47
Thai-Style Mackerel	18
Tomato Sorbet	13
Tuna with Sesame Seeds and Ginger	20
Vegetable Pilaf with Almonds	26
Vegetable Stock	22
White Beans in Tomato Sauce	33
Wholewheat Pasta with Chunky Tomato Sauce	46
Winter Soup	3

Editorial Coordination: Merehurst Limited
Cookery Editors: Polly Boyd, Jenni Fleetwood, Katie Swallow
Editorial Assistant: Sheridan Packer
Production Manager: Sheridan Carter
Layout and Finished Art: Stephen Joesph
Cover Photography: David Gill
Cover Design: Maggie Aldred

Published by J.B. Fairfax Press Pty Limited
80-82 McLachlan Avenue
Rushcutters Bay 2011
A.C.N. 003 738 430
Formatted by J.B. Fairfax Press Pty Limited
Printed by Toppan Printing Co, Singapore

JBFP 251 A/UK
Includes Index
ISBN 1 86343 120 9
ISBN 1 86343 116 0 (Set)

DISTRIBUTION AND SALES ENQUIRIES
Australia: J.B. Fairfax Press Pty Limited
Ph: (02) 361 6366 Fax: (02) 360 6262
United Kingdom: J.B. Fairfax Press Limited
Ph (0933) 402330   Fax (02) 402234